Feathers

Illustrated by Yoko Matsuoka

by Sandy Stream

Feathers. By Sandy Stream
Illustrated by Yoko Matsuoka
Edited by Tomoko Matsuoka

ISBN 978-0-9739481-7-2

On a Personal Note

We spend our lives avoiding pain. We always move away from it, avoiding it because it simply does not feel good.

But trying to keep something contained takes a tremendous amount of energy, and the body's resources get used up—leading to unease and illness.

Why go *towards* pain, you might ask?

Why not? If it is actually there, then explore the truth. Let the truth win over everything.

Sandy Stream

Based on *many* true stories

Once upon a time there was a nest with three little eggs.

One summer day, the first egg hatched and Sparky was born. The next day, the second egg hatched and Mama called her precious bird "Feathers" because he was as light as a feather.

The next day, the last egg hatched, and Flex was born. Feathers and his family lived in a beautiful world. It had rainbows and sunshine and beautiful trees.

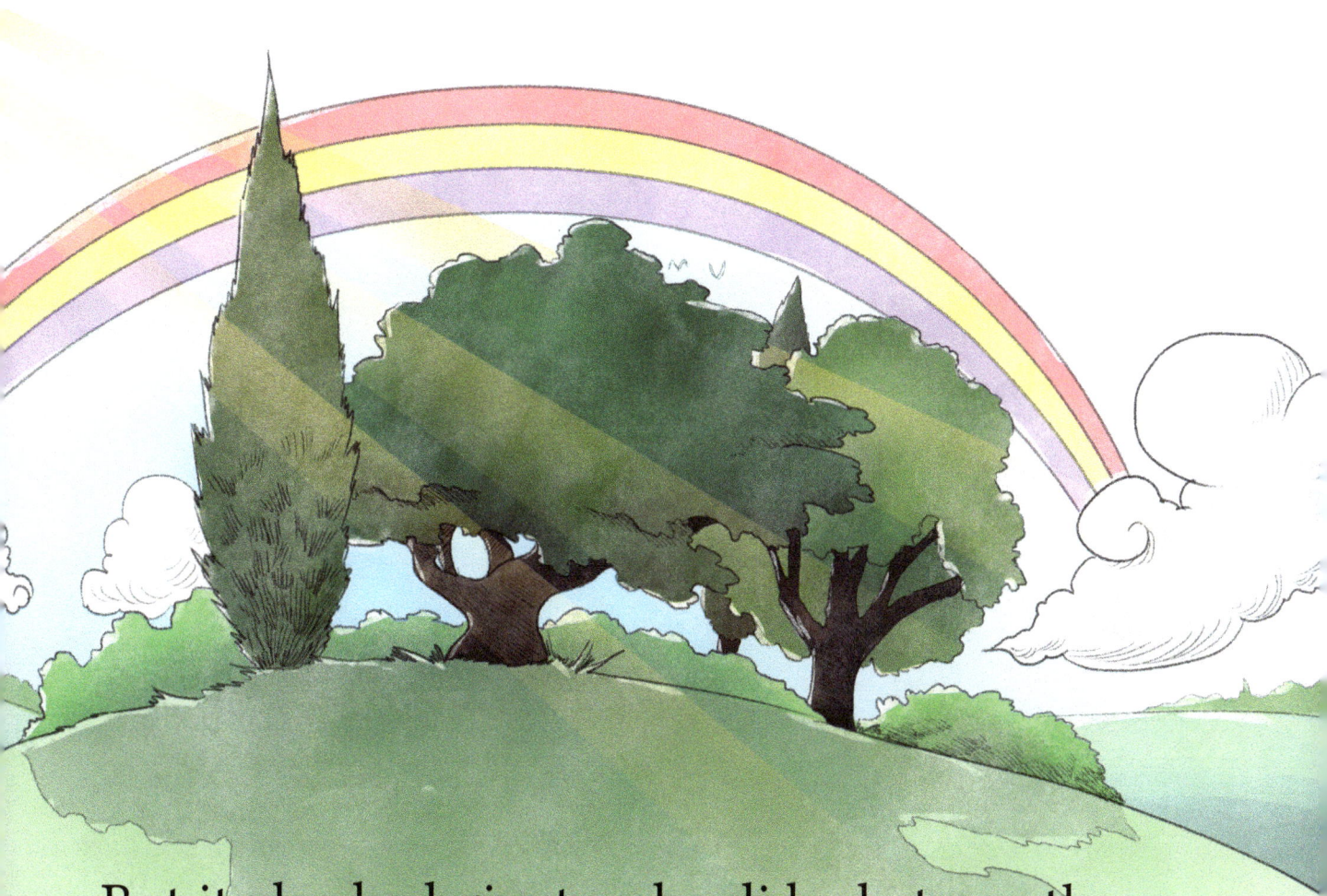

But it also had giants who did whatever they wanted. Feathers had never seen a giant before.

Every day, mama brought worms and love to the nest, filling Feathers' heart more and more each day.

But then one terrible day, Sparky was taken by a giant and Mama followed to try to bring Sparky back.

Feathers hardly ever saw his mama after that day. She was always flying off somewhere. Feathers had an empty space in his heart.

Feathers knew his heart had a hole in it, but he got used to it being there. He didn't tell any of the other little birds about it. He didn't want anyone to know how different he was.

When he was older, he left his nest. He spent a lot of time with his many friends.

Feathers thought that they might be able to fill the hole in his heart. But his friends could not fill the hole in his heart.

He tried to eat lots of worms and wild berries. But they could not fill the hole in his heart.

He tried to ignore and accept the hole in his heart. But it only grew darker and darker and felt heavier and heavier.

So he went to see the wise owl at the edge of the forest. The owl smiled and said:
"Go fly to the top of the highest mountain and you will see that the answer is in you."

On his way to the mountain, he met a beautiful bird named Lilac. She was so lovely and she smelled like flowers. He thought this must be the reason the owl had sent him this way.

She loved Feathers and shared her heart with him. But even with her, he felt all alone. And he knew that he didn't have a full heart to give her, so Feathers went back to see the owl.

"I met a lovely girl but I still feel all alone.
I tried to feel better, but it didn't work."

The owl answered:
"Who told you to try to feel better? Does
the wind try to feel better? Go to the top of
the highest mountain and the answer will
be in you."

Feathers returned to Lilac and told her what the owl had said. Lilac gave Feathers a peck and let him go on his journey.

up.

up,

Feathers flew up,

When he got to the top of the mountain,
he realized that there were no other birds
around at all. He was all alone. His heart felt
very heavy.

It was very windy on top of the mountain.
He felt the wind moving his feathers...
...and he understood.
The answer is in you—Feathers!
Be like the wind...light as a feather!

Feathers had an idea. He would try to
breathe some wind in so he could become
lighter.

He waited until morning so he could breathe
in sunshine-filled air... He tried to breathe in
sunny air every day for thirty days.

But it did not change the hole in his heart.
So Feathers went back to the owl and told
him how breathing sunny air had not
worked.

The owl smiled:
"Who told you to breathe in sunny air?
Does the wind choose the air?"
So Feathers went back to the mountain and
tried to breathe sunny air *and* nighttime air.

He started to breathe—opening his chest, his lungs, and then his stomach. He tried to breathe slowly; he tried to breathe deeply. Air went into his chest, lungs, and filled his stomach, but it did not help his heart.

He went back to the owl and told him
how he had tried so hard but nothing had
worked. The owl told him:
"Does the wind *try* to breathe?
It just breathes! Just breathe!"

Feathers understood. He went back to the mountain and stopped trying to feel better. He closed his eyes and let air enter his body naturally.

He took another breath. He felt the air enter and he let it in. He watched how it moved inside him, and how it started to move him inside...

The air made a small space inside his heart,
which gave the black hole more room to move.
Then the hole started to get even *bigger*!
He let the air in and didn't try to stop it from
growing. He didn't push it down; or hold it.
He didn't try to shrink it...he simply let it
spread.

The black hole spread and spread and spread. Feathers watched it, felt it fully, and let it move on its own without trying to control it...

It grew and grew, and he felt a sharp pain in his heart. It was deep sadness.
He was unable to move.
The hole spread over his entire body and Feathers was now as dark as the night sky.
He was as sad as anyone could ever be in this world...

...And then, with a gentle silence, the hole
continued its movement out of his body and
into the dark night sky...

It went over the valley, over the river...
...and up into the dark universe where it
was absorbed.

Then he felt Lilac's scent envelop him...
Feather's heart healed and expanded into the
space left behind by the hole.
It was fuller yet lighter.

In the morning, Feathers awoke feeling fresh and new—and as light as a feather.

He glided down the winds of the great big mountain, ready to join Lilac and his world.

The now

The River Series

Sparky Can Fly
Sparky's Mama
Tweets and Hurricanes
Feathers
Flex
Roots
The River

www.RiverSpeaks.com

www.ingramcontent.com/pod-product-compliance
Lightning Source LLC
Chambersburg PA
CBHW051618030426
42334CB00030B/3243